Under  Warm Sea

by Dawn McMillan

Harcourt
SCHOOL PUBLISHERS

ISBN 10: 0-15-351274-1
ISBN 13: 978-0-15-351274-2

Ordering Options
ISBN 10: 0-15-351211-3 (Grade 1 Advanced Collection)
ISBN 13: 978-0-15-351211-7 (Grade 1 Advanced Collection)
ISBN 10: 0-15-358024-0 (package of 5)
ISBN 13: 978-0-15-358024-6 (package of 5)

Coral is made from lots of
little animals.
A lot of coral grows in
warm water.
Some coral grows in cold water.

Some coral looks like a rock.
Some coral looks like a forest
under the water.
Some coral looks more like
a ball.

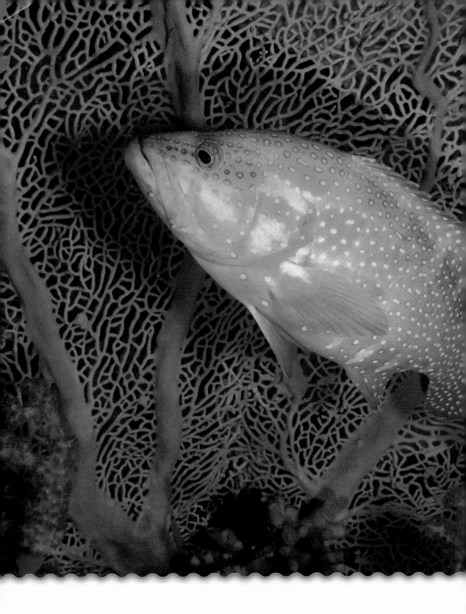

Some fish live in the coral.
Some fish are red like the coral.

4

Big fish look for their food
in the coral.
They look for little fish that
live there.
The big fish swim up and
back, up and back!

Swim very fast, little fish!
The big fish will see you,
and they will get you!

The little fish swim into
the coral.
They are hidden from the
big fish.
They can have a rest.

Soon the big fish swim off.
Now the little fish can come
out again.